Introduction

Terrific Table Toppers is just the book you need to create usable gorgeous toppers for any table. You can set the mood or theme for dinners or events with one of these 9 toppers. Any topper from this diverse group would also make the perfect handmade gift for friends and family. Now you have the patterns you need to impress everyone with your quilting skills!

Pick any of these beautiful designs, plug in your choice of fabrics and colors, and simply stitch it up. You'll find yourself going back to this book to make more beautiful toppers since the designs inside are not only fun and easy, but also timeless, to fit in with any decor or season. You just need a desire to make them and some fabrics you love. This is a must-have-on-hand book for any quilter who is looking for clear instructions for great projects that can be made in her or his spare time. It's destined to be your go-to book for fast and easy projects to adorn your table.

Enjoy!

Table of Contents

Strips Galore Table Topper

Put those leftover strips to use. Simply sort until you like the color combination and then strip-piece them. It's much easier than it looks.

Designed & Quilted by Carolyn S. Vagts

Skill Level
Confident Beginner

Finished Size
Topper Size: 30" diameter

Materials
- 21 assorted 2½" by fabric width precut strips for A
- ⅝ yard black solid includes binding. If using purchased bias tape, then only ⅜ yard is needed.
- Backing to size
- Batting to size
- Template material
- 3⅛ yards black bias tape (optional)
- Thread
- Basic sewing tools and supplies

Project Notes
Read all instructions before beginning this project.

Stitch right sides together using a ¼" seam allowance unless otherwise specified.

Materials and cutting lists assume 40" of usable fabric width for yardage.

Cutting
Prepare wedge and circle templates using provided patterns.

From black solid:
- Cut 3 (1½" by fabric width) B strips.
- Cut 2 circles using prepared template.
- Cut 2¼" bias strips to total 110" when seamed together for binding. (Omit if using purchased bias tape.)

Completing the Topper
1. Sort A strips into three groups of seven strips each.

2. Select one group of A strips and one B strip and sew together on the long sides as shown in Figure 1 to make an A-B strip set; press seams in one direction. Repeat to make a total of three A-B strip sets, changing the position of B in each strip set.

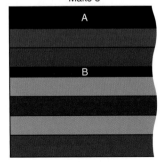

A-B Strip Set
Make 3

Figure 1

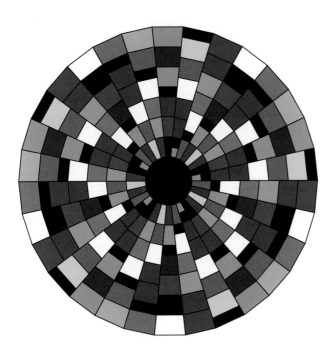

Strips Galore Table Topper
Placement Diagram 29" diameter

3. Referring to Figure 2, position the placement line on the wedge template with a seam line on the right side of an A-B strip set, making sure the entire wedge is on the fabric, and cut 10 wedges from each strip set, reversing the position of the wedge for every other cut. Repeat to cut a total of 30 wedges.

Cut 30 wedges

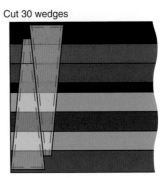

Figure 2

4. Arrange and stitch two wedges together on the long side as shown in Figure 3; press seam open.

Figure 3

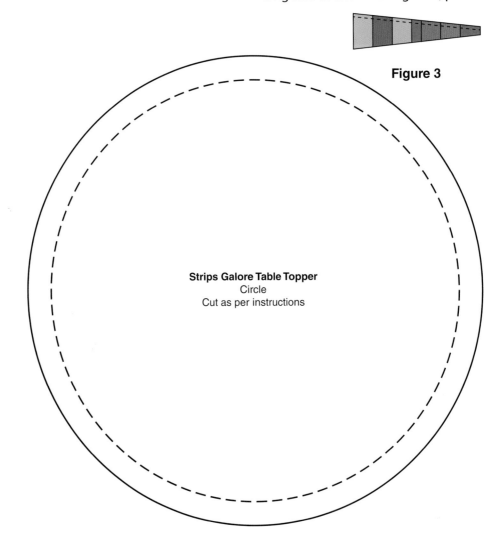

Strips Galore Table Topper
Circle
Cut as per instructions

5. In the same manner, stitch all wedges together to form a pieced circle; press.

6. With right sides together, stitch black solid circles together. Referring to Figure 4, cut a slash in the middle of one circle only and turn right side out through slash; press. Whipstitch opening closed to complete the center circle.

Figure 4

7. Position center circle over center opening of pieced circle; hand- or machine-stitch in place to complete the top.

8. Layer and quilt as desired. Prepare bias binding, unless using bias tape, and bind referring to Quilting Basics on page 47. Sample topper was machine-quilted with a free-motion meander in strips and a swirl motif in the center circle. ●

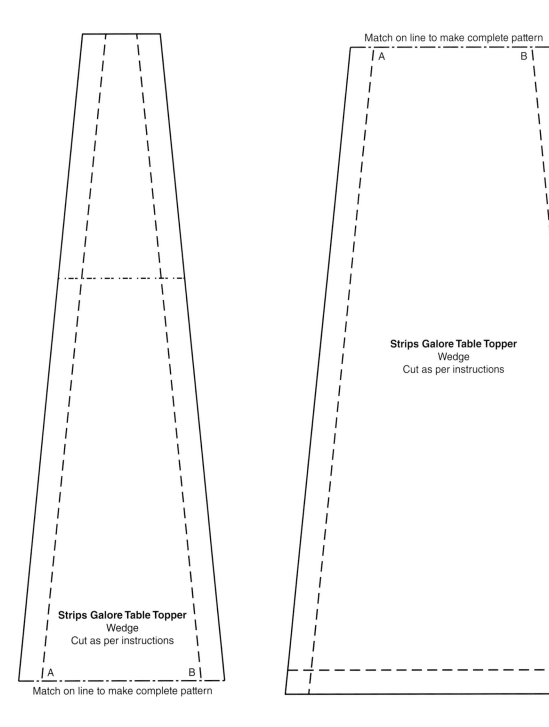

Strips Galore Table Topper
Wedge
Cut as per instructions

A   B

Match on line to make complete pattern

Match on line to make complete pattern

A   B

Strips Galore Table Topper
Wedge
Cut as per instructions

Fireside

These tiny Pineapple blocks can easily be made
with fabric scraps to match any decor.

Designed & Quilted by Connie Kauffman

Skill Level
Intermediate

Finished Sizes
Topper Size: approximately 20" x 20"
Block Size: 4¾" x 4¾"
Number of Blocks: 9

Materials
- Scraps of red tonal, prints and solids
  at least 1¼" wide—label as B
- Scraps of light-to-medium prints at least
  1¼" wide—label as C
- Scraps of medium tonals at least 2" square
- ¼ yard red dot
- ⅓ yard black solid
- Backing to size
- Batting to size
- Paper-piecing paper
- Thread
- Basic sewing tools and supplies

Project Notes
Read all instructions before beginning this project.

Stitch right sides together using a ¼" seam
allowance unless otherwise specified.

Materials and cutting lists assume 40" of usable
fabric width for yardage.

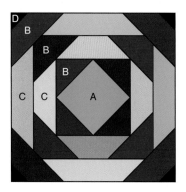

Pineapple
4³/₄" x 4³/₄" Finished Block
Make 9

Cutting

From medium tonal scraps:
- Cut 9 (2") A squares.

From red dot:
- Cut 4 (4") E squares.

From black solid:
- Cut 1 (7" by fabric width) strip.
  Subcut strip into 1 (7") F square and 18 (1½")
  D squares; cut the F square on both diagonals
  to make 4 F triangles and the D squares in half
  on 1 diagonal to make 36 D triangles.

Completing the Blocks
1. Make nine copies of the provided paper-
piecing pattern.

2. Referring to Paper Piecing on page 10 and the
block drawing for fabric placement, use A, B, C and
D pieces to make nine Pineapple blocks.

Prairie Points

Easy to make, prairie points are a fun addition to quilt edges or even as insertions in blocks or borders to give your quilt depth and movement with a sawtooth detail.

1. Fold a square in half diagonally (Figure A) and press.

Figure A   **Figure B**

2. Fold in half again and press referring to Figure B.

3. To add prairie points to a seam, pin the first point to the seam edge and then tuck the consecutive prairie point ends between the folds of the previous prairie points and pin in place (Figure C). Baste the prairie points in place.

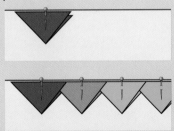

Figure C

To use prairie points as a binding embellishment on quilted projects:

4. After quilting and trimming the quilt top, batting and backing even, add prairie points around the quilt edges referring to step 3, with prairie points pointed toward the quilt center. Baste to hold in place. ***Note:*** *Adjust how far the points are inserted together for even spacing.* Finish quilt with binding.

Completing the Topper

1. Referring to Figure 1, arrange and stitch the Pineapple blocks into three rows of three blocks each; press. Sew the rows together to complete the topper center; press.

Figure 1

2. Referring to Prairie Points, fold an E square twice on the diagonal to make a prairie point; press. Repeat to make a total of four prairie points.

3. Center a prairie point on top of each side of the topper center with raw edges aligned as shown in Figure 2; baste in place.

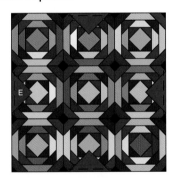

Figure 2

4. Referring to Figure 3, center an F triangle right side down over each prairie point, aligning long raw edges; baste in place.

Figure 3

5. Flip the layered units out, away from the center; press seams toward the center.

6. Layer the batting with backing right side up and top right side down. Stitch ¼" around all sides, leaving a 3" opening in one F edge. Trim excess batting and backing. Trim corners and clip inside corners. Turn right side out through the opening; press, making sure prairie points are flat and edges smooth.

7. Turn the edges of the opening in and hand-stitch closed.

8. Quilt as desired. Sample topper was machine-quilted in the ditch of seams using clear monofilament. ●

Fireside
Assembly Diagram Approximately 20" x 20"

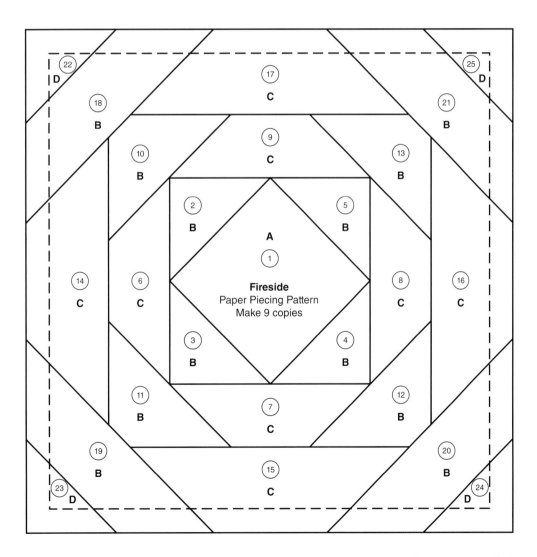

Fireside
Paper Piecing Pattern
Make 9 copies

Paper Piecing

Paper piecing allows a quilter to make blocks with odd-shaped and/or small pieces and more precise corners. Fabric pieces are sewn together onto the reverse side of a paper-piecing pattern, and then the paper is carefully removed when the block is completed. You may have to rethink how you piece when using this technique, and it does require a little more yardage.

1. Make same-size copies of the paper-piecing pattern as directed in the pattern. There are several choices in transparent papers as well as water-soluble papers that can be used, which are available at your local office supply store, quilt shop or online. Some papers can be used in your printer.

2. Cut out the patterns, leaving a margin around the outside bold lines as shown in Figure A. All patterns are reversed on the paper copies. Pattern color choices can be written in each numbered space on the marked side of each copy.

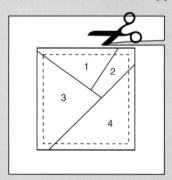

Figure A

3. When cutting fabric for paper piecing, the pieces do not have to be the exact size and shape of the area to be covered. Cut fabric pieces the general shape and ¼"–½" larger than the design area to be covered. This makes paper piecing a good way to use up scraps.

4. With the printed side of the pattern facing you, fold along each line of the pattern as shown in Figure B, creasing the stitching lines. This will help in trimming the fabric seam allowances and in removing the paper when you are finished stitching. *Note: You can also machine-stitch along the lines with a basting stitch and no thread to perforate the paper.*

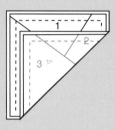 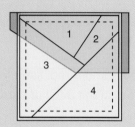

Figure B   **Figure C**

5. Turn the paper pattern over with the unmarked side facing you and position fabric indicated on pattern right side up over the space marked 1. Hold the paper up to a window or over a light box to make sure that the fabric overlaps all sides of space 1 at least ¼" as shown in Figure C from the printed side of the pattern. Pin to hold fabric in place. *Note: You can also use a light touch of glue stick. Too much glue will make the paper difficult to remove.*

6. Turn the paper over with the right side of the paper facing you, and fold the paper along the lines between sections 1 and 2. Trim fabric to about ¼" from the folded edge as shown in Figure D.

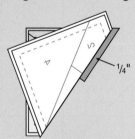

Figure D

7. Place the second fabric indicated right sides together with first piece. Fabric edges should be even along line between spaces 1 and 2 as shown in Figure E. Fold fabric over and check to see if second fabric piece will cover space 2.

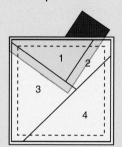

Figure E

8. With the right side of the paper facing you, hold fabric pieces together and stitch along the line between spaces 1 and 2 as shown in Figure F using a very small stitch length (18–20 stitches per inch). *Note: Using a smaller stitch length will make removing paper easier because it creates a tear line at the seam. Always begin and end seam by sewing two to three stitches beyond the line. You do not need to backstitch. Start sewing at the solid outside line of the pattern when the beginning of the seam is at the edge of the pattern.*

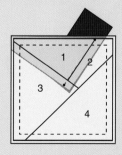 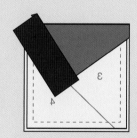

Figure F   **Figure G**

9. Turn the pattern over, flip the second fabric back and finger-press as shown in Figure G.

10. Continue trimming and sewing pieces in numerical order until the pattern is completely covered. Make sure pieces along the outer edge extend past the solid line to allow for a ¼" seam allowance as shown in Figure H.

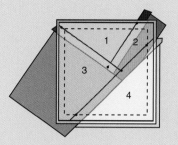

Figure H

11. When the whole block is sewn, press the block and trim all excess fabric from the block along the outside-edge solid line of the paper pattern as shown in Figure I.

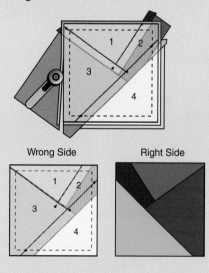

Wrong Side   Right Side

Figure I

12. After stitching blocks together, carefully remove the backing paper from completed blocks and press seams. You can also staystitch ⅛" from the outer edge of the completed block. Carefully remove backing paper and press seams. Then complete quilt top assembly.

Study in Blue Dresden Topper

Put those fat quarters to use! This cute table topper can be made with just four fat quarters and a backing fabric. It's a quick and easy project.

Designed & Quilted by Carolyn S. Vagts

Skill Level
Confident Beginner

Finished Size
Topper Size: 22" diameter

Materials
- 4 assorted blue batik fat quarters
- Backing to size
- Batting to size
- Template material
- Thread
- Basic sewing tools and supplies

Project Notes
Read all instructions before beginning this project.

Stitch right sides together using a ¼" seam allowance unless otherwise specified.

Materials and cutting lists assume 20" of usable fabric width for fat quarters.

Cutting
Prepare Dresden blade and circle templates using provided patterns.

From blue fat quarters:
- Using prepared template, cut 3 Dresden blades from each fat quarter for a total of 12 blades.
- Cut 2 circles using prepared template.

Completing the Topper

1. Position Dresden blades into a pleasing color arrangement. When satisfied with the placement, stitch two blades together on the long side as shown in Figure 1; press seam open.

Figure 1

2. In the same manner, stitch all blades together to form a pieced circle as shown in Figure 2; press.

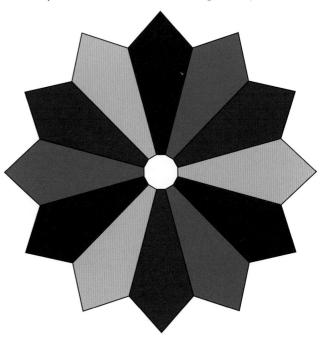

Figure 2

3. With right sides together, stitch center circles together. Referring to Figure 3, cut a slash in the middle of one circle only and turn right side out through slash; press. Whipstitch opening closed to complete the center circle.

Figure 3

4. Position center circle over center opening of blade pieced circle and machine- or hand-stitch in place to complete the top.

5. Layer the batting with backing right side up and top right side down. Stitch ¼" around all sides of the top, leaving a 2½" opening in one side. Trim excess batting and backing. Trim corners and clip inside corners. Turn right side out through the opening; press, turning in the edges of the opening.

6. Hand-stitch opening closed.

7. Quilt as desired. Sample topper was outline-quilted ¼" from outer edge and stitched with a leafy swirl in each blade. ●

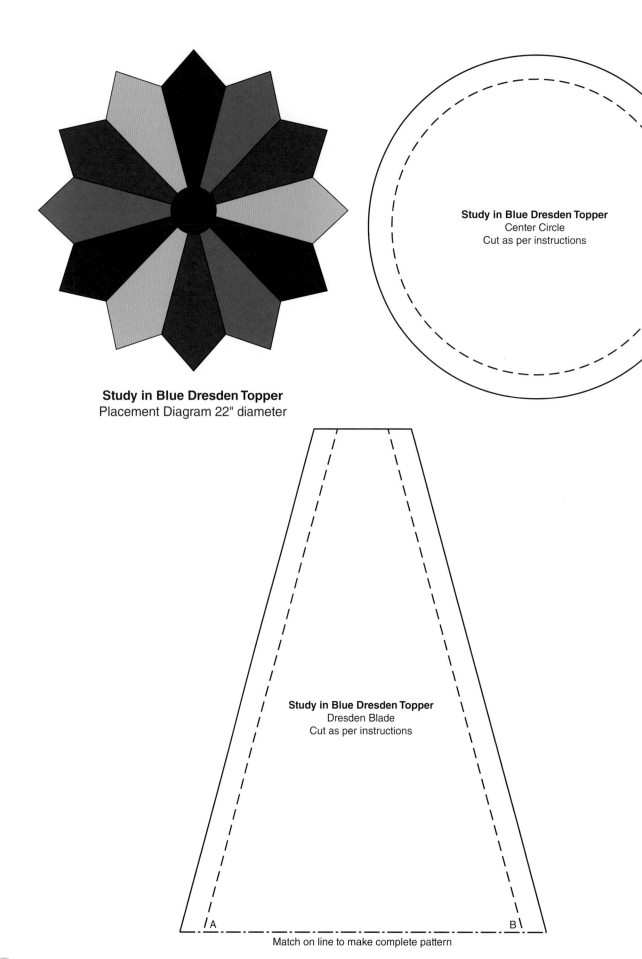

Study in Blue Dresden Topper
Placement Diagram 22" diameter

Study in Blue Dresden Topper
Center Circle
Cut as per instructions

Study in Blue Dresden Topper
Dresden Blade
Cut as per instructions

A   B

Match on line to make complete pattern

Match on line to make complete pattern

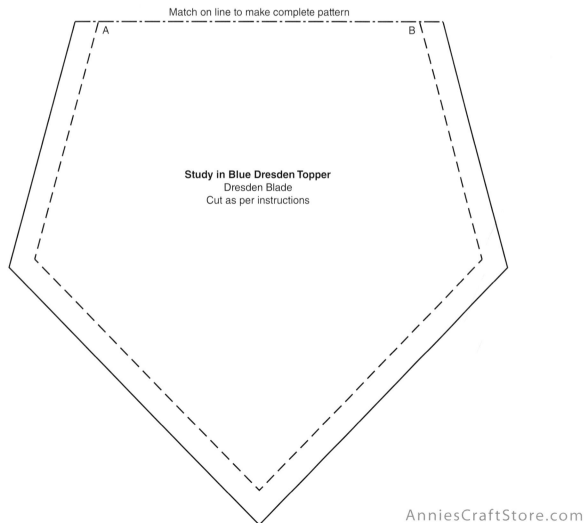

A   B

Study in Blue Dresden Topper
Dresden Blade
Cut as per instructions

Spring Fling

Want to brighten up your table and cheer up a special meal?
This gorgeous diamond will do just that—and impress your guests.

Designed & Quilted by Susan Smith

Skill Level
Confident Beginner

Finished Size
Table Topper Size: 25½" x 43½"

Materials
- Fat quarter each of 8–10 coordinating prints in a variety of scales and colors
- ⅓ yard coordinating tonal
- ⅞ yard focal print
- Backing to size
- Batting to size
- 60-degree equilateral triangle ruler
- Long straightedge
- 18" x 30" parchment or semitransparent pattern paper
- Craft knife
- Thread
- Basic sewing tools and supplies

Project Notes
Read all instructions before beginning this project.

Stitch right sides together using a ¼" seam allowance unless otherwise specified.

Materials and cutting lists assume 40" of usable fabric width for yardage and 20" for fat quarters.

Cutting

From each fat quarter:
- Cut 2 each 1¼" x 20" B, 1½" x 20" C, 1¾" x 20" D and 2" x 20" E strips for a total of 16–20 each B, C, D and E strips.

From coordinating tonal:
- Cut 3 (2¼" by fabric width) binding strips.

From focal print:
Make a template for the center diamond by folding the 18" x 30" rectangle of parchment or pattern paper into quarters. Measure and mark 8" from the folded corner on the short side and 13¾" on the long side as shown in Figure 1. Draw a diagonal line connecting the two marks. Using a craft knife and long straightedge, cut along the drawn line. Unfold the template. Each side should measure 15¹⁵⁄₁₆.

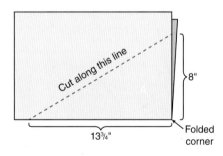

Figure 1

- Cut 1 A diamond using the template keeping parallel sides of template aligned with the cut edge of the fabric.

Completing the Triangle Units

1. Select one each B, C, D and E strip. Randomly sew together on the long sides to make a strip set; press. Repeat to make a total of 10 strip sets. *Note: Not all strips are used.*

2. Referring to Figure 2 and using the 60-degree triangle ruler, cut a total of 32 (5"-tall) triangle units from the strip sets, rotating the ruler on the strip set to maximize fabric usage.

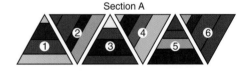

Cut 32
Triangle Units

5"

Figure 2

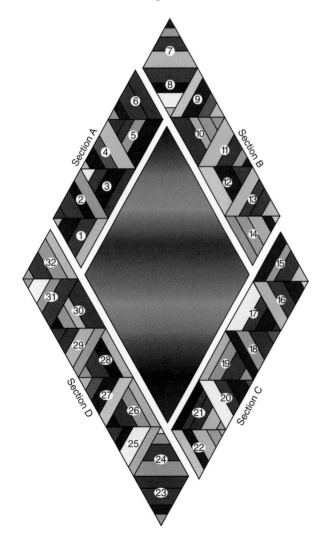

Spring Fling
Assembly Diagram 25½" x 43½"

Completing the Topper

1. Lay out triangle units around the A diamond, rotating units so that the stripes go in different directions. When satisfied with the arrangement, number triangle units from 1 to 32.

2. Arrange and stitch triangle units 1–6 as shown in Figure 3 to make section A; press seams in one direction.

Section A

Figure 3

3. Repeat step 2, joining units 7–14 to make section B, units 15–22 to make Section C and units 23–32 to make Section D.

4. Referring to the Assembly Diagram, stitch each section to the A diamond in alphabetical order to complete the top; press.

5. Layer, quilt as desired and bind referring to Quilting Basics on page 47. Sample table topper was machine-quilted with outline quilting of each floral motif in the center section and straight line quilting in the triangle units. ●

Just Bloom Fresh

Top your table with beautiful baskets of flowers
for the perfect touch of elegance.

Designed & Quilted by CJ Behling

Skill Level
Confident Beginner

Finished Sizes
Topper Size: 48" x 48"
Block Size: 17" x 17"
Number of Blocks: 4

Materials
- Fat eighth each lime solid and orange tonal
- ¼ yard medium gray solid
- ⅓ yard light green print
- ⅝ yard dark green tonal
- ⅝ yard dark gray solid
- ⅝ yard aqua print
- ⅞ yard dark gray tonal
- 1¼ yards white tonal
- Backing to size
- Batting to size
- 1 package medium gray single-fold bias tape
- Template material
- Fusible web with paper release
- Air- or water-soluble marking pen
- Thread
- Basic sewing tools and supplies

Project Notes
Read all instructions before beginning this project.

Stitch right sides together using a ¼" seam allowance unless otherwise specified.

Materials and cutting lists assume 40" of usable fabric width for yardage.

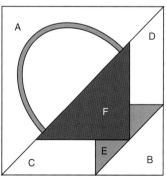

Basket
17" x 17" Finished Block
Make 4

Cutting

From medium gray solid:
- Cut 1 (3⅞" by fabric width) strip.
  Subcut strip into 4 (3⅞") squares; cut each square in half on 1 diagonal to make 8 E triangles.

From light green print:
- Cut 1 (6½" by fabric width) strip.
  Subcut strip into 4 (6½") H squares.
- Cut 1 (4¾" by fabric width) strip.
  Subcut strip into 4 (4¾") G squares.

From dark green tonal:
- Cut 1 (12½" by fabric width) strip.
  Subcut strip into 8 (4¾" x 12½") L rectangles.

From dark gray solid:
- Cut 6 (2¼" by fabric width) binding strips.

From aqua print:
- Cut 1 (6⅞" by fabric width) strip.
  Subcut strip into 4 (6⅞") M squares, 4 (2⅝") O squares and 4 (2¼") J squares; cut M and O squares in half on 1 diagonal to make 8 M and 8 O triangles.
- Cut 1 (5⅛" by fabric width) strip.
  Subcut strip into 4 (5⅛") squares; cut each square in half on 1 diagonal to make 8 N triangles.

From dark gray tonal:
- Cut 1 (11⅞" by fabric width) strip.
  Subcut strip into 2 (11⅞") squares; cut each square in half on 1 diagonal to make 4 F triangles.
- Cut 5 (2¼" by fabric width) strips.
  Subcut strips into 16 (2¼" x 4¾") I and 8 (2¼" x 12½") K strips.

From white tonal:
- Cut 1 (17⅞" by fabric width) strip.
  Subcut strip into 2 (17⅞") squares. Cut each square in half on 1 diagonal to make 4 A triangles.

- Cut 1 (6⅞" by fabric width) strip.
  Subcut strip into 2 (6⅞") squares. Cut each square on 1 diagonal to make 4 B triangles.
- Cut 1 (11⅞" by fabric width) strip.
  Subcut strip into 8 (3½" x 11⅞") rectangles. Referring to Figure 1, trim 1 end of each rectangle at a 45-degree angle to make 4 C and 4 D pieces.

Figure 1

Completing the Blocks

1. Fold each A triangle in half and lightly crease to mark the centerline. Prepare a template for the basket handle referring to the placement guide. Place the template on an A triangle, aligning the edges with the creased centerline and one long edge of the triangle as indicated on the pattern. Mark along the curved edge of the template using an air- or water-soluble marking pen. Flip the template over and mark the curve on the remaining half of A to complete the basket handle placement. Repeat to mark each A triangle.

2. Open one folded side of the bias tape and, with right sides together, pin the fold crease on the drawn line on A so the bulk of the tape is outside the marked arc and will cover the drawn line when folded down. Stitch in place along the fold crease of bias tape.

3. Fold tape down and pin in place, distributing any fullness on the inner side of the arc. Edge-stitch with a reduced straight stitch or narrow zigzag to secure as shown in Figure 2. Repeat with all four A triangles.

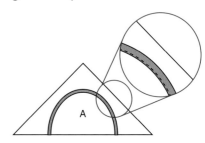

Figure 2

4. Referring to Figure 3 for orientation, stitch an E triangle to the square end of a C piece to make a C-E unit; press. Repeat to make a total of four C-E units. Repeat to make four D-E units, again referring to Figure 3.

C-E Unit
Make 4

D-E Unit
Make 4

Figure 3

5. Arrange and stitch a C-E and D-E unit to each side of an F triangle as shown in Figure 4 to make a basket row; press. Repeat to make a total of four basket rows.

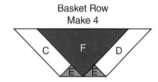

Basket Row
Make 4

Figure 4

6. Referring to Figure 5, sew a B triangle to the short side of a basket row to make a basket triangle; press. Repeat to make a total of four basket triangles.

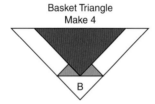

Basket Triangle
Make 4

Figure 5

7. Stitch an A triangle and basket triangle together on long sides referring to the block drawing to make a Basket block; press. Repeat to make a total of four Basket blocks.

8. Prepare appliqué shapes for small and large leaves, flowers and flower centers using the full-size patterns given, referring to Raw-Edge Fusible Appliqué on page 24 and the list below for the number to cut from each fabric.

- Aqua Print: 16 small leaves
- Dark Green Tonal: 8 large leaves
- Pale Green Solid: 4 flowers
- Orange Tonal: 4 flower centers

9. Arrange one flower with flower center, two large leaves and four small leaves as shown in Figure 6 on each basket block. When satisfied with the arrangement, fuse in place.

Figure 6

10. Machine-stitch around all appliqué shapes using matching thread.

Completing the Corner Units

1. Referring to Figure 7, stitch a G square and I strip together to make a G-I unit; press. Repeat to make a total of four G-I units.

G-I Unit
Make 4

Figure 7

2. Arrange and sew a J square on one end of an I strip as shown in Figure 8 to make an I-J unit; press. Repeat to make a total of four I-J units. Repeat with I strips and O triangles to make four each I-O and reversed I-O units, again referring to Figure 8.

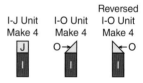

I-J Unit
Make 4

I-O Unit
Make 4

Reversed
I-O Unit
Make 4

Figure 8

3. Referring to Figure 9, arrange and join one each G-I and I-J units to make a G-I-J unit; press. Repeat to make a total of four G-I-J units.

G-I-J Unit
Make 4

Figure 9

4. Arrange and sew one each L and K strip together on the long side to make a K-L unit as shown in Figure 10; press. Repeat to make a total of eight K-L units.

K-L Unit
Make 8

Figure 10

5. Referring to Figure 11a, sew an M triangle to one side of an H square; press. Sew a second M triangle to an adjacent side of H (Figure 11b) to make an H-M unit; press. Repeat to make a total of four H-M units.

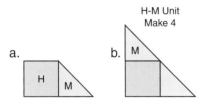

H-M Unit
Make 4

Figure 11

6. Arrange and join a K-L unit and an H-M unit as shown in Figure 12; press. Repeat to make a total of four units.

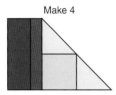

Make 4

Figure 12

7. Referring to Figure 13, arrange and sew a G-I-J unit to one end of a K-L unit; press. Repeat to make a total of four units.

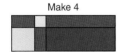

Make 4

Figure 13

8. Join one each unit from steps 6 and 7, one each I-O and reversed I-O unit, and two N triangles as shown in Figure 14 to make a corner unit; press. Repeat to make a total of four corner units.

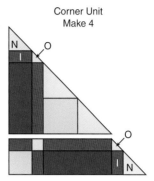

Corner Unit
Make 4

Figure 14

Completing the Topper

1. Referring to the Assembly Diagram, arrange and sew the basket blocks into two rows of two blocks each; press. Sew rows together to complete the topper center.

2. Center and stitch a corner unit to each side of the topper center to complete the top; press.

3. Layer, quilt as desired and bind referring to Quilting Basics on page 47. Sample topper was machine-quilted with a free-motion meander around the appliqués in the center section and with straight line stitching in the corner units. ●

Just Bloom Fresh
Assembly Diagram 48" x 48"

Raw-Edge Fusible Appliqué

One of the easiest ways to appliqué is the raw-edge fusible-web method. Paper-backed fusible web individual pieces are fused to the wrong side of specified fabrics, cut out and then fused together in a motif or individually to a foundation fabric, where they are machine-stitched in place.

Choosing Appliqué Fabrics

Depending on the appliqué, you may want to consider using batiks. Batik is a much tighter weave and, because of the manufacturing process, does not fray. If you are thinking about using regular quilting cottons, be sure to stitch your raw-edge appliqués with blanket/buttonhole stitches instead of a straight stitch.

Cutting Appliqué Pieces

1. Fusible appliqué shapes should be reversed for this technique.

2. Trace the appliqué shapes onto the paper side of paper-backed fusible web. Leave at least ¼" between shapes. Cut out shapes leaving a margin around traced lines. *Note: If doing several identical appliqués, trace reversed shapes onto template material to make reusable templates for tracing shapes onto the fusible web.*

3. Follow manufacturer's instructions and fuse shapes to wrong side of fabric as indicated on pattern for color and number to cut.

4. Cut out appliqué shapes on traced lines. Remove paper backing from shapes.

5. Again following fusible web manufacturer's instructions, arrange and fuse pieces to quilt referring to quilt pattern. Or fuse together shapes on top of an appliqué ironing mat to make an appliqué motif that can then be fused to the quilt.

Stitching Appliqué Edges

Machine-stitch appliqué edges to secure the appliqués in place and help finish the raw edges with matching or invisible thread (Photo 1). ***Note:*** *To show stitching, all samples have been stitched with contrasting thread.*

Straight stitch

Buttonhole or blanket stitch

Photo 1

Invisible thread can be used to stitch appliqués down when using the blanket or straight stitches. Do not use it for the satin stitch. Definitely practice with invisible thread before using it on your quilt; it can sometimes be difficult to work with.

A short, narrow buttonhole or blanket stitch is most commonly used (Photo 2). Your machine manual may also refer to this as an appliqué stitch. Be sure to stitch next to the appliqué edge with the stitch catching the appliqué.

Photo 2

Practice turning inside and outside corners on scrap fabric before stitching appliqué pieces. Learn how your machine stitches so that you can make the pivot points smooth.

1. To stitch outer corners, stitch to the edge of the corner and stop with needle in the fabric at the corner point. Pivot to the next side of the corner and continue to sew (Photo 3). You will get a box on an outside corner.

Photo 3

2. To stitch inner corners, pivot at the inner point with needle in fabric (Photo 4). You will see a Y shape in the corner.

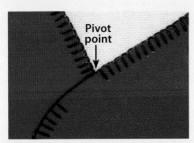

Pivot point

Photo 4

3. You can also use a machine straight stitch. Turn corners in the same manner, stitching to the corners and pivoting with needle in down position (Photo 5).

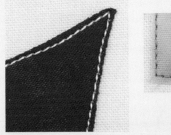

Photo 5

General Appliqué Tips

1. Use a light- to medium-weight stabilizer behind an appliqué to keep the fabric from puckering during machine stitching (Photo 6).

Photo 6

2. To reduce the stiffness of a finished appliqué, cut out the center of the fusible-web shape, leaving ¼"–½" inside the pattern line. This gives a border of adhesive to fuse to the background and leaves the center soft and easy to quilt.

3. If an appliqué fabric is so light-colored or thin that the background fabric shows through, fuse a lightweight interfacing to the wrong side of the fabric. You can also fuse a piece of the appliqué fabric to a matching piece, wrong sides together, and then apply the fusible web with a drawn pattern to one side.

Just Bloom Fresh
Flower
Cut as per instructions

Just Bloom Fresh
Small Leaf
Cut as per instructions

Just Bloom Fresh
Large Leaf
Cut as per instructions

Just Bloom Fresh
Flower Center
Cut as per instructions

Just Bloom Fresh
Placement Guide for Basket Handle
A

Place on creased centerline

Place on long edge of A

Apple a Day

Add a fun twist to your table tonight. Apple pie, anyone?

Designed & Quilted by Tricia Lynn Maloney

Skill Level
Confident Beginner

Finished Sizes
Topper Size: 24" x 24"
Block Size: 7" x 7"
Number of Blocks: 4

Materials
- Scraps of brown and green tonals
- 4 assorted red 10" precut squares
- ⅜ yard white solid
- ¾ yard red tonal
- Backing to size
- Batting to size
- Template material
- Fusible web with paper release
- Thread
- Basic sewing tools and supplies

Project Notes
Read all instructions before beginning this project.

Stitch right sides together using a ¼" seam allowance unless otherwise specified.

Materials and cutting lists assume 40" of usable fabric width for yardage.

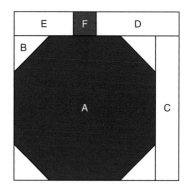

Apple
7" x 7" Finished Block
Make 4

Cutting

From brown tonal:
- Cut 4 (1½") F squares.

From red precut squares:
- Cut 4 (6½") A squares.

From white solid:
- Cut 3 (1½" by fabric width) strips.
  Subcut strips into 16 (1½") B squares and 4 (1½" x 6½") C, 4 (1½" x 4") D and 4 (1½" x 3") E strips.
- Cut 2 (2½" by fabric width) strips.
  Subcut strips into 2 each 2½" x 14½" G and 2½" x 18½" H strips.

From red tonal:
- Cut 3 (3½" by fabric width) strips.
  Subcut strips into 2 each 3½" x 18½" I and 3½" x 22½" J strips.
- Cut 3 (2½" by fabric width) binding strips.

Completing the Blocks

1. Draw a diagonal line on the wrong side of each B square.

2. Position a B square right sides together on one corner of an A square and stitch on the drawn line as shown in Figure 1a. Cut ¼" past the stitching line and press B open (Figure 1b). Repeat to add a B square on each corner of A (Figure 1c) to make an A-B unit. Repeat to make a total of four A-B units.

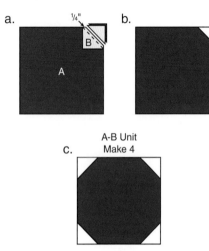

Figure 1

3. Referring to Figure 2, arrange and stitch a C strip to the right edge of an A-B unit to make an A-B-C unit; press. Repeat to make a total of four A-B-C units.

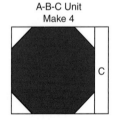

Figure 2

4. Sew an F square between a D strip and E strip to make a D-E-F unit as shown in Figure 3; press. Repeat to make a total of four D-E-F units.

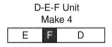

Figure 3

5. Referring to the block drawing, stitch a D-E-F unit to the top of an A-B-C unit to complete one Apple block; press. Repeat to make a total of four blocks.

Completing the Topper

1. Arrange and stitch the blocks into two rows of two blocks each as shown in Figure 4; press. Sew rows together to complete the topper center; press.

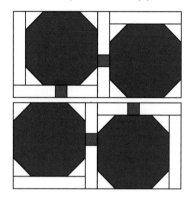

Figure 4

2. Referring to the Assembly Diagram, stitch G strips to opposite sides of the topper center and H strips to the top and bottom; press.

3. Stitch I strips to opposite sides of the quilt center and J strips to the top and bottom to complete the quilt top; press.

4. Referring to Raw-Edge Fusible Appliqué on page 24, prepare four leaves from the green tonal fabric using the full-size template provided.

5. Position a leaf on each Apple block referring to the Assembly Diagram for positioning. When satisfied with the placement, fuse in place.

6. If desired, machine blanket-stitch around appliqué shapes using matching thread.
Note: *Leaves in the sample topper were stitched in place in the machine-quilting process.*

7. Layer, quilt as desired and bind referring to Quilting Basics on page 47. Sample topper was machine-quilted with a free-motion meander in the center section and arcs in the outer border. ●

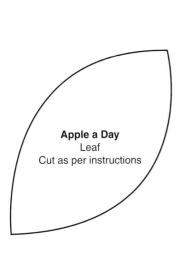

Apple a Day
Leaf
Cut as per instructions

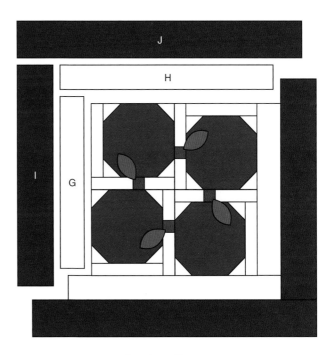

Apple a Day
Assembly Diagram 24" x 24"

Falling Leaves Topper

Turn a collection of favorite autumn fabrics into a scrappy topper that will warm up any table.

Designed & Quilted by Nancy Walhout Recker

Skill Level

Confident Beginner

Finished Size

Topper Size: 44" x 44"
Block Size: 9" x 9"
Number of Blocks: 16

Materials

- ¼ yard light red tonal
- ¼ yard dark green print
- ¼ yard light brown tonal
- ⅓ yard orange tonal
- ⅓ yard medium red tonal
- ⅜ yard light green tonal
- ½ yard medium brown tonal
- ¾ yard light gray tonal
- 1¼ yards dark brown tonal
- Backing to size
- Batting to size
- Thread
- Basic sewing tools and supplies

Project Notes

Read all instructions before beginning this project.

Stitch right sides together using a ¼" seam allowance unless otherwise specified.

Materials and cutting lists assume 40" of usable fabric width for yardage.

Cutting

From light red tonal:

- Cut 1 (3⅞" by fabric width) strip.
    Subcut strip into 2 (3⅞") D squares and 4 (2⅝") R squares; cut each square in half on 1 diagonal to make 4 D and 8 R triangles.

From dark green print:

- Cut 1 (5¼" by fabric width) strip.
    Subcut strip into 2 (5¼") DD squares and 4 (3½") K squares; cut DD squares on both diagonals to make 8 DD triangles.

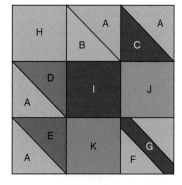

Leaf
9" x 9" Finished Block
Make 4

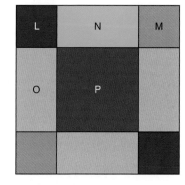

Nine-Patch
9" x 9" Finished Block
Make 8

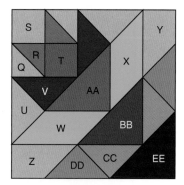

Basket
9" x 9" Finished Block
Make 4

From light brown tonal:
- Cut 1 (4⅜" by fabric width) strip.
  Subcut strip into 2 (4⅜") AA squares, 2 (3⅞")
  E squares and 4 (2¼") T squares; cut AA and
  E squares in half on 1 diagonal to make 4 each
  AA and EE triangles.

From orange tonal:
- Cut 1 (3¾" by fabric width) strip.
  Subcut strip into 2 (3¾") CC squares, 4 (3½")
  J squares and 2 (2¾") M squares; cut CC squares
  on both diagonals to make 8 CC triangles.
- Cut 1 (2¾" by fabric width) strip.
  Subcut strip into 14 (2¾") M squares to total
  16 M squares.

From medium red tonal:
- Cut 1 (4¾" by fabric width) strip.
  Subcut strip into 2 (4¾") V squares and 2 (2¾")
  L squares; cut V squares on both diagonals to
  make 8 V triangles.
- Cut 1 (2¾" by fabric width) strip.
  Subcut strip into 14 (2¾") L squares to total
  16 L squares.

From light green tonal:
- Cut 1 (3⅞" by fabric width) strip.
  Subcut strip into 2 (3⅞") B squares and
  2 (2¼" x 6½") W/X strips; cut B squares in half
  on 1 diagonal to make 4 B triangles.
- Cut 1 (2¾" by fabric width) strip.
  Subcut strip into 8 (2¾" x 5") N strips.
- Cut 1 (2¼" by fabric width) strip.
  Subcut strip into 6 (2¼" x 6½") W/X strips to
  total 8 W/X strips; referring to Figure 1, trim
  both ends of each strip to make 4 each W and
  X pieces.

Figure 1

From medium brown tonal:
- Cut 1 (5" by fabric width) strip.
  Subcut strip into 8 (5") P squares.
- Cut 1 (4½" by fabric width) strip.
  Subcut strip into 4 (4½") GG squares and
  2 (4⅜") BB squares; cut BB squares in half
  on 1 diagonal to make 4 BB triangles.
- Cut 1 (3⅞" by fabric width) strip.
  Subcut strip into 2 (3⅞") C squares, 4 (3½") I squares
  and 4 (1¼" x 5") G strips; cut C squares in half
  on 1 diagonal to make 4 C triangles.

From light gray tonal:
- Cut 1 (4¾" by fabric width) strip.
  Subcut strip into 2 (4¾") U squares and 4 (2⅝")
  Q squares; cut U squares on both diagonals
  to make 8 U triangles and Q squares in half
  on 1 diagonal to make 8 Q triangles.
- Cut 1 (2½" by fabric width) strip.
  Subcut strip into 8 (2½" x 4⅜") strips; referring
  to Figure 2, trim 1 end of each strip to make
  4 Y and 4 Z pieces.

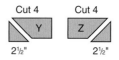

Figure 2

- Cut 1 (3⅞" by fabric width) strip.
  Subcut strip into 8 (3⅞") A squares and 4 (2¼")
  S squares; cut A squares in half on 1 diagonal
  to make 16 A triangles.
- Cut 1 (3½" by fabric width) strip.
  Subcut strip into 8 (3½") squares; cut 4 squares
  in half on 1 diagonal to make 8 F triangles
  and label remaining 4 squares as H.
- Cut 3 (2¾" by fabric width) strips.
  Subcut strips into 24 (2¾" x 5") O strips.

From dark brown tonal:
- Cut 4 (4½" by fabric width) strips.
  Subcut strips into 4 (4½" x 36½") FF strips.
- Cut 1 (4⅜" by fabric width) strip.
  Subcut strip into 2 (4⅜") squares; cut each square
  in half on 1 diagonal to make 4 EE triangles.
- Cut 5 (2¼" by fabric width) binding strips.

Completing the Blocks

Leaf Block

1. Arrange and stitch one each A and B triangle together on the long edges to make an A-B unit as shown in Figure 3; press. Repeat to make a total of four A-B units.

A-B Unit
Make 4

Figure 3

2. Referring to Figure 4, repeat step 1 to make four each A-C, A-D and A-E units.

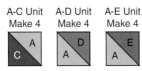

A-C Unit   A-D Unit   A-E Unit
Make 4   Make 4   Make 4

Figure 4

3. Center and stitch F triangles to opposite sides of G strip as shown in Figure 5 to make an F-G unit; press. Trim unit to 3½" square. Repeat to make a total of four F-G units.

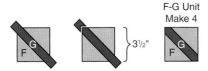

F-G Unit
Make 4

Figure 5

4. Referring to Figure 6, arrange one each A-B, A-C, A-D, A-E and F-G unit and one each H, I, J and K square into three rows of three units/squares each. Stitch into rows and stitch rows together to complete one Leaf block; press. Repeat to make a total of four Leaf blocks.

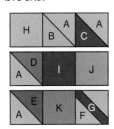

Figure 6

Nine-Patch Block

1. Arrange L, M, N, O and P pieces into three rows of three pieces each as shown in Figure 7. Stitch pieces into rows and stitch rows together to complete one Nine-Patch block; press. Repeat to make a total of eight Nine-Patch blocks.

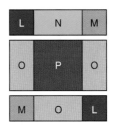

Figure 7

Basket Block

1. Referring to Figure 8, repeat step 1 of Leaf block to make eight Q-R units.

Q-R Unit
Make 8

Figure 8

2. Arrange and stitch one each S and T square and two Q-R units into two rows as shown in Figure 9. Stitch rows together to complete one Q-R-S-T unit; press. Repeat to make a total of four Q-R-S-T units.

Q-R-S-T Unit
Make 4

Figure 9

3. Referring to Figure 10, arrange and stitch U and V triangles into four each U-V units and reversed U-V units; press.

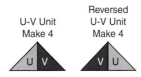

U-V Unit   Reversed
Make 4   U-V Unit
              Make 4

Figure 10

4. Arrange and stitch one each U-V and reversed U-V unit on adjacent sides of a Q-R-S-T unit as shown in Figure 11; press. Repeat to make a total of four top corner units.

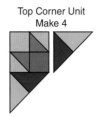

Top Corner Unit
Make 4

Figure 11

5. Referring to Figure 12, arrange and join Z, W, AA, X and Y pieces to make a center row. Repeat to make a total of four center rows.

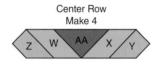

Center Row
Make 4

Figure 12

6. Arrange and stitch a CC triangle to opposite short sides of a BB triangle to make a BB-CC unit as shown in Figure 13; press. Repeat to make a total of four BB-CC units.

BB-CC Unit
Make 4

Figure 13

7. Referring to Figure 14, arrange and stitch DD triangles to opposite ends of a BB-CC unit and the long side of an EE triangle to the CC side; press. Repeat to make a total of four bottom corner units.

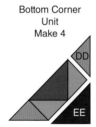

Bottom Corner
Unit
Make 4

Figure 14

8. Arrange and stitch top and bottom corner units on opposite sides of a center row as shown in Figure 15 to complete one Basket block; press. Repeat to make a total of four Basket blocks.

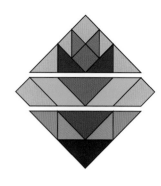

Figure 15

Completing the Topper

1. Referring to the Assembly Diagram, arrange and stitch blocks into four rows of four blocks each; press. Sew rows together to complete the topper center; press.

2. Sew FF strips to opposite sides of the topper center; press.

3. Sew GG squares to both ends of the remaining two FF strips to make two border units; press. Stitch border units to the top and bottom of the topper center to complete the top; press.

4. Layer, quilt as desired and bind referring to Quilting Basics on page 47. Sample topper was machine-quilted with a free-motion meander in the center section and straight line stitching in the borders. ●

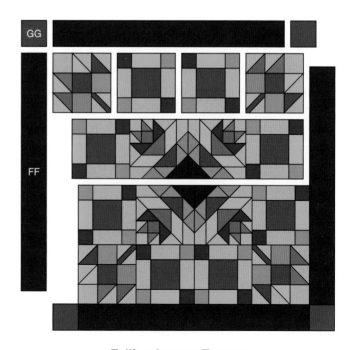

Falling Leaves Topper
Assembly Diagram 44" x 44"

North Woods Table Topper

Turn Log Cabin blocks into majestic pine trees for a woodsy look.

Designed & Quilted by Connie Rand

Skill Level
Confident Beginner

Finished Sizes
Topper Size: 51" x 51"
Block Size: 6" x 6"
Number of Blocks: 24

Materials
- 1 (2½" by fabric width) K strip brown tonal
- 1⅛ yards light blue batik
- 3 yards total assorted green prints and tonals
- Backing to size
- Batting to size
- Template material
- Thread
- Basic sewing tools and supplies

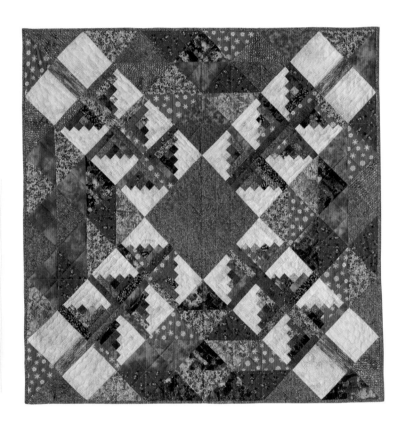

Project Notes
Read all instructions before beginning this project.

Stitch right sides together using a ¼" seam allowance unless otherwise specified.

Materials and cutting lists assume 40" of usable fabric width for yardage.

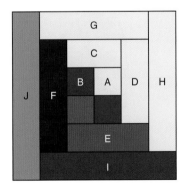

Log Cabin
6" x 6" Finished Block
Make 24

Cutting

From light blue batik:

- Cut 11 (1½" by fabric width) strips.
  Subcut strips into 24 each 1½" A squares and 1½" x 2½" C, 1½" x 3½" D, 1½" x 4½" G and 1½" x 5½" H rectangles.
- Cut 2 (5½" by fabric width) L strips.

From assorted green prints & tonals:

- Prepare a template for the N/O triangle using full-size pattern given. Cut 48 N triangles and 24 O triangles, paying close attention to positioning of fabric grain for each triangle.
- Cut 1 (12½") M square.
- Cut 72 (1½") B squares, and 24 each 1½" x 3½" E, 1½" x 4½" F, 1½" x 5½" I and 1½" x 6½" J rectangles.
- Cut 6 (2¼" by fabric width) binding strips.

Completing the Blocks

1. Sew an A square to a B square to make an A-B unit; press. Join two B squares and then sew to the A-B unit to make a four-patch unit, as shown in Figure 1; press. Repeat to make a total of 24 four-patch units.

Four-Patch Unit
Make 24

Figure 1

2. Referring to Figure 2, stitch C and then D to the A-B sides of a four-patch unit; press toward the strip. Add E and F to complete one round of strips; press.

Figure 2

3. Continue adding G–J strips in alphabetical order in a clockwise orientation to make one Log Cabin block as shown in Figure 3; press.

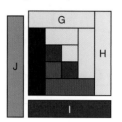

Figure 3

4. Repeat steps 2 and 3 to make a total of 24 Log Cabin blocks.

Completing the Topper

1. Join two Log Cabin blocks referring to Figure 4 to make a two-block unit; press. Repeat to make 12 two-block units.

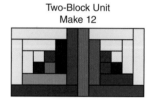

Two-Block Unit
Make 12

Figure 4

2. Referring to Figure 5, join three two-block units to make a tree unit; press. Repeat to make a total of four tree units.

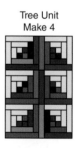

Tree Unit
Make 4

Figure 5

3. Sew a K strip lengthwise between two L strips to make a strip set; press. Subcut into four 6½" x 12½" trunk units as shown in Figure 6.

Trunk Unit
Cut 4
6½"

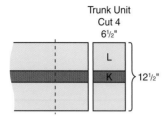

12½"

Figure 6

4. Sew a trunk unit to each tree unit as shown in Figure 7; press. Sew two O triangles together on the short sides and sew to the trunk end of the tree unit to make one corner strip, again referring to Figure 7; press. Repeat to make a total of four corner strips.

Corner Strip
Make 4

Figure 7

5. Stitch the M square between two corner strips to make the center row referring to the Assembly Diagram; press.

6. Sew two N triangles together along the long diagonal edges to make an N unit; press. Repeat to make a total of 24 N units.

7. Join six N units in rows and add four O triangles as shown in Figure 8 to make a side unit; press. Repeat to make a total of four side units.

Side Unit
Make 4

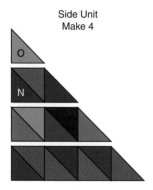

Figure 8

8. Referring to the Assembly Diagram, sew a side unit to opposite long sides of the two remaining corner strips to make two corner units; press. Join the corner units with the center row to complete the top; press.

9. Layer, quilt as desired and bind referring to Quilting Basics on page 47. Sample topper was machine-stitched in the ditch of seams in the green sections of the Log Cabin block and with wavy lines in the blue sections. It was straight-line quilted in the center square and triangles. ●

North Woods Table Topper
Assembly Diagram 51" x 51"

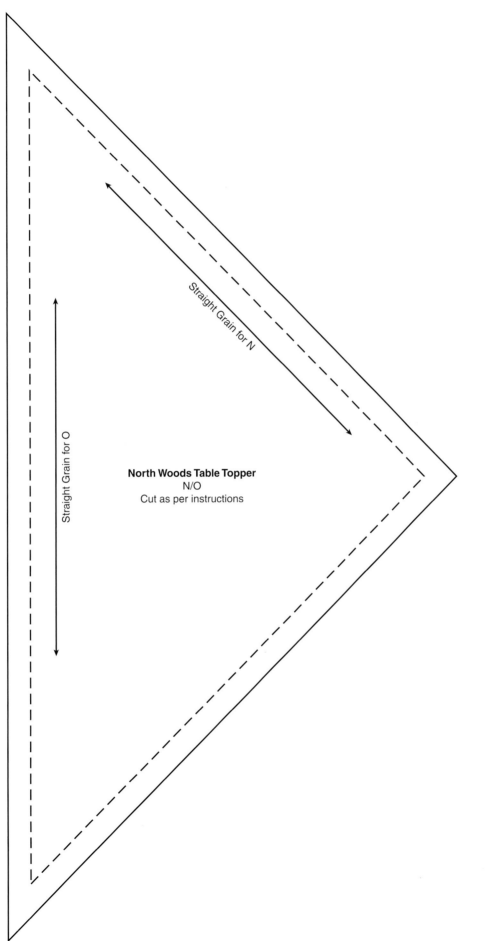

Straight Grain for N

Straight Grain for O

North Woods Table Topper
N/O
Cut as per instructions

Poinsettia Topper

Add a touch of the holiday season to any table.

Designed & Quilted by Denise Russell of Pieced Brain

Skill Level
Beginner

Finished Sizes
Topper Size: 21½" x 21½"
Block Size: 19½" x 19½"
Number of Blocks: 1

Materials
- ⅓ yard poinsettia print
- ⅓ yard green tonal
- ⅓ yard black tonal
- ⅓ yard white-with-red-dot
- ⅝ yard red dot
- Backing to size
- Batting to size
- Template material
- Fusible web with paper release
- Thread
- Basic sewing tools and supplies

Project Notes
Read all instructions before beginning this project.

Stitch right sides together using a ¼" seam allowance unless otherwise specified.

Materials and cutting lists assume 41" of usable fabric width for yardage.

Poinsettia
19½" x 19½" Finished Block
Make 1

Cutting

From poinsettia print:
- Cut 1 (2½" by fabric width) strip.
  Subcut strip into 8 (2½") A squares and 8 (2⅛") L squares.
- Cut 1 (4⅛" by fabric width) strip.
  Subcut strip into 4 (4⅛") E squares.

From green tonal:
- Cut 1 (2½" by fabric width) strip.
  Subcut strip into 8 (2½") D squares and 8 (2⅛") M squares.
- Cut 1 (4⅛" by fabric width) strip.
  Subcut strip into 4 (4⅛") H squares.

From black tonal:
- Cut 1 (2½" by fabric width) strip.
  Subcut strip into 8 (2½") B squares and
  8 (2⅛") K squares.
- Cut 1 (4⅛" by fabric width) strip.
  Subcut strip into 4 (4⅛") F squares.

From white-with-red-dot:
- Cut 1 (2½" by fabric width) strip.
  Subcut strip into 4 (2½") C squares, 4 (2⅛" x 3¾")
  J strips and 4 (2⅛") I squares.
- Cut 1 (4⅛" by fabric width) strip.
  Subcut strip into 8 (4⅛") G squares.

From red dot:
- Cut 3 (1½" by fabric width) strips.
  Subcut strips into 2 each 1½" x 20" N and
  1½" x 22" O strips.
- Cut 3 (2¼" by fabric width) binding strips.

Completing the Block

1. Draw a diagonal line on the wrong side of the A and B squares.

2. With right sides together, pair a marked A and D square together and stitch ¼" on both sides of the drawn line as shown in Figure 1. Cut on the drawn line and press open to make two A-D units. Repeat to make a total of 12 A-D units.

Figure 1

3. Referring to Figure 2, repeat step 2 to make a total of four A-B units, four B-D units and eight B-C units.

Figure 2

4. Draw a diagonal line on the wrong side of two E and the G squares.

5. Repeat step 2 using E, F, G and H squares to make four each E-H, E-G, and G-H units and eight F-G units as shown in Figure 3.

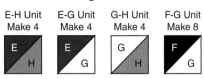

Figure 3

6. Referring to Figure 4, arrange and stitch one each G-H and E-G unit to make an E-G-H unit and two F-G units to make an F-G-G unit; press seam open. Repeat to make a total of four units each.

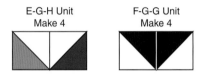

Figure 4

7. Arrange and stitch E-H units into two rows of two units each as shown in Figure 5; press. Sew rows together to make an E-H square; press.

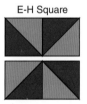

Figure 5

8. Prepare one circle using the full-size pattern given and referring to Raw-Edge Fusible Appliqué on page 24.

9. Center circle on the E-H square and fuse in place.

10. Machine blanket-stitch around appliqué shape using matching thread.

11. Referring to Figure 6, join I squares and A-D units to make two each A-D-I and reversed A-D-I units; press.

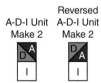

Figure 6

12. Arrange and stitch a J strip to one side of the A-D-I and reversed A-D-I units to make two each A-D-I-J and reversed A-D-I-J units as shown in Figure 7; press.

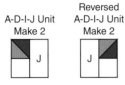

A-D-I-J Unit
Make 2

Reversed
A-D-I-J Unit
Make 2

Figure 7

13. Referring to Figure 8, arrange and stitch one each B-C and A-B unit and one each K and L square into two rows; press. Sew rows together to complete one L four-patch unit; press. Repeat to make a total of four units.

L Four-Patch Unit
Make 4

Figure 8

14. Arrange and stitch one each B-C and B-D unit and one each K and M square into two rows as shown in Figure 9; press. Sew rows together to complete one M four-patch unit; press. Repeat to make a total of four units.

M Four-Patch Unit
Make 4

Figure 9

15. Referring to Figure 10, arrange and stitch two A-D units and one each L and M square into two rows of two units each; press. Sew rows together to complete one A-D four-patch unit; press. Repeat to make a total of four units.

A-D Four-Patch Unit
Make 4

Figure 10

16. Arrange and sew one each E-G-H and F-G-G unit on opposite sides of the E-H square to make a center row as shown in Figure 11; press.

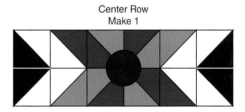

Center Row
Make 1

Figure 11

17. Referring to Figure 12, arrange and sew one M four-patch unit and a reversed A-D-I-J unit to one side and an A-D-I-J unit and an L four-patch unit to the opposite side of an E-G-H unit to make an inner row; press. Repeat to make two inner rows.

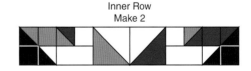

Inner Row
Make 2

Figure 12

18. Arrange and stitch one each A-D and L four-patch unit to one side and one each A-D and M four-patch unit to the opposite side of a F-G-G unit to make an outer row as shown in Figure 13; press. Repeat to make two outer rows.

Outer Row
Make 2

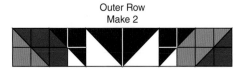

Figure 13

19. Referring to the block drawing, arrange and stitch inner rows to opposite sides of the center row; press. Arrange and stitch outer rows in place to complete the block; press.

Completing the Topper

1. Referring to the Assembly Diagram, stitch N strips to opposite sides of the block and O strips to the top and bottom to complete the top; press.

2. Layer, quilt as desired and bind referring to Quilting Basics on page 47. Sample topper was machine-quilted with a free-motion holly meander in the center section and holly motif in the borders. ●

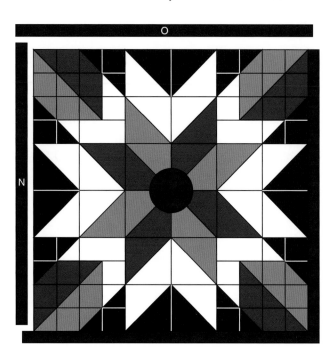

Poinsettia Topper
Assembly Diagram 21½" x 21½"

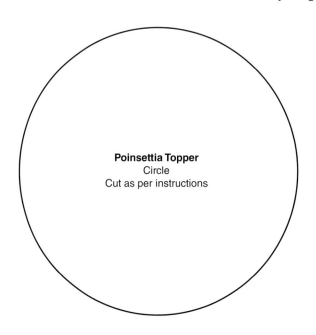

Poinsettia Topper
Circle
Cut as per instructions

Quilting Basics

The following is a reference guide. For more information, consult a comprehensive quilting book.

Quilt Backing & Batting

We suggest that you cut your backing and batting 8" larger than the finished quilt-top size. If preparing the backing from standard-width fabrics, remove the selvages and sew two or three lengths together; press seams open. If using 108"-wide fabric, trim to size on the straight grain of the fabric.

Prepare batting the same size as your backing. You can purchase prepackaged sizes or battings by the yard and trim to size.

Quilting

1. Press quilt top on both sides and trim all loose threads.
2. Make a quilt sandwich by layering the backing right side down, batting and quilt top centered right side up on flat surface and smooth out. Pin or baste layers together to hold.
3. Mark quilting design on quilt top and quilt as desired by hand or machine. **Note:** *If you are sending your quilt to a professional quilter, contact them for specifics about preparing your quilt for quilting.*
4. When quilting is complete, remove pins or basting. Trim batting and backing edges even with raw edges of quilt top.

Binding the Quilt

1. Join binding strips on short ends with diagonal seams to make one long strip; trim seams to ¼" and press seams open (Figure A).

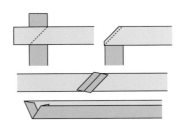

Figure A

2. Fold 1" of one short end to wrong side and press. Fold the binding strip in half with wrong sides together along length, again referring to Figure A; press.
3. Starting about 3" from the folded short end, sew binding to quilt top edges, matching raw edges and using a ¼" seam. Stop stitching ¼" from corner and backstitch (Figure B).

Figure B

4. Fold binding up at a 45-degree angle to seam and then down even with quilt edges, forming a pleat at corner, referring to Figure C.

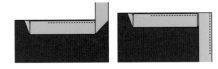

Figure C

5. Resume stitching from corner edge as shown in Figure C, down quilt side, backstitching ¼" from next corner. Repeat, mitering all corners, stitching to within 3" of starting point.
6. Trim binding end long enough to tuck inside starting end and complete stitching (Figure D).

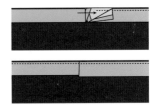

Figure D

7. Fold binding to quilt back and stitch in place by hand or machine to complete your quilt.

Special Thanks

Please join us in thanking the talented designers whose work is featured in this collection.

CJ Behling
Just Bloom Fresh, page 19

Connie Kauffman
Fireside, page 6

Tricia Lynn Maloney
Apple a Day, page 28

Connie Rand
North Woods Table Topper, page 37

Nancy Walhout Recker
Falling Leaves Topper, page 32

Denise Russell of Pieced Brain
Poinsettia Topper, page 42

Susan Smith
Spring Fling, page 16

Carolyn S. Vagts
Strips Galore Table Topper, page 2
Study in Blue Dresden Topper, page 12

Supplies

We would like to thank the following manufacturers who provided materials to our designers to make sample projects for this book.

Strips Galore Table Topper, page 2: Precut strips from Hoffman and Tuscany; 80/20 cotton/wool blend batting from Hobbs.

Fireside, page 6: Soft & Bright batting from The Warm Company.

Study in Blue Dresden Topper, page 12: Cold Spell batik collection from Moda and Tuscany; 80/20 cotton/wool blend batting from Hobbs.

Poinsettia Topper, page 42: Poinsettia & Pine fabric collection from Maywood Studio.

Published by Annie's, 306 East Parr Road, Berne, IN 46711. Printed in USA. Copyright © 2018, 2019 Annie's. All rights reserved. This publication may not be reproduced in part or in whole without written permission from the publisher.

RETAIL STORES: If you would like to carry this publication or any other Annie's publications, visit AnniesWSL.com.

Every effort has been made to ensure that the instructions in this publication are complete and accurate. We cannot, however, take responsibility for human error, typographical mistakes or variations in individual work. Please visit AnniesCustomerService.com to check for pattern updates.

ISBN: 978-1-59012-922-7

456789